WORLD RELIGIONS

FACTS ABOUT

JUDAISM

Alison Cooper

rosen publishing's
rosen
central

New York

Published in 2011 by The Rosen Publishing Group Inc.
29 East 21st Street, New York, NY 10010

Copyright © 2011 Wayland/
The Rosen Publishing Group, Inc.

First Edition

Original designer and illustrator: Celia Hart
Layout for this edition: Jane Hawkins
Consultant: Johnathan Gorsky

Library of Congress Cataloging-in-Publication Data

Cooper, Alison, 1967-
  Facts about Judaism / Alison Cooper. — 1st ed.
     p. cm. — (World religions)
  Includes bibliographical references and index.
  ISBN 978-1-61532-323-4 (library binding)
  ISBN 978-1-61532-326-5 (paperback)
  ISBN 978-1-61532-335-7 (6-pack)
  1. Judaism. I. Title.
  BM562.C66 2011
  296—dc22
                                    2009052263

Photographs:
Front cover, Corbis; Andes Press Agency, pp. 8 41(b) (Carlos Reyes-Manzo);
Architectural Association, p. 21(b) (John Ross); MS Kennicott 1 Folio 30R, Bodleain
Library Oxford; Anat Rotem-Braun, Jerusalem, pp. 15(1), 29(t), 31(c); Werner Braun,
Jerusalem, p. 33(b); Bridgeman Art Libraray, pp. 13(t) Giraudon / "Jacob's Dream" by
Ludovico Cardi da Cigoli (1559–1613), Musee des Beaux-Arts, Nancy 14 "Moses and
the Tablets of the Law" by Hermensz van Rijn Rembrandt (1606-69), Dahlem Staatlicke
Gemaldegalerie, Berlin, 34 "Saul Listening to David Playing the Harp" by Erasmus
Quellinus (1607–78), Museum of Fine Arts, Budapest, 41(t) "The Jewish Marriage" by
Ilex Bellers (20th Century), Private Collection; British Library, Oriental & India Office
Collections, pp. 12, 13(c), 40; Camera Press, p. 31(t) (Y Braun); Circa Photo Library,
pp. 25(t), 43 (Barrie Searle); Kuperard Ltd, p. 20; Hulton Deutsch Collection, p. 27(br);
Israeli Post Office, Philatetic Serivce, p. 34(r); Henry Jacobs, p. 35(b); Michael
Le Poer Trench, p. 13(b); Rony Oren, The Animated Haggadah, Scopus
Films (London) Ltd, p. 33(t) (Trevor Clifford); Photo Researchers Inc,
NY, p. 9; Zev Radovan, Jerusalem, pp. 27(bl), 31(b), 32, 37; Peter
Sanders Photography, p. 36; Traditions Mail Order, endpapers
(Trevor Clifford), 39(t) from the original in the Israeli Museum
(Jeffrey Gendler); Stewart Weir, pp. 17(br), 23, 24, 25(b); 38,
39(b); Westhill RE Centre, pp. 15(r), 16, 17(t), 30; Zefa Pictures,
pp. 17(bl), 18, 19, 21(t), 22, 27, 28, 29(b), 35(t).

Endpapers: This hand-painted silk Shabbat cloth shows the
seven foods harvested in Israel: wheat, barley, grapes, olives,
pomegranates, dates, and figs. (by Yair Emanuel, Emanuel
Studio, Jerusalem)

Manufactured in China
CPSIA Compliance Information: Batch #WAS0102YA: For Further Information
contact Rosen Publishing, New York, New York at 1-800-237-9932

CONTENTS

WHO ARE THE JEWS?

Jews live in many countries around the world. There are different ideas about what makes people Jewish. For example, some Jews believe you have to have a Jewish mother in order to be Jewish, but others believe you are Jewish if either of your parents is Jewish. The laws of the Jewish religion, Judaism, are very important to many Jews, but some Jews do not practice Judaism at all.

◀ Kibbutz

In Israel, some Jews live in farm villages. One type of farm village is called a kibbutz. The adults who live on the kibbutz share the work on the farm. They also take turns to work in the kitchens, the houses, and the laundry. Children work together, go to school together, and play together.

Towns and Cities ▶

Many large towns and cities have areas where Jewish stores, schools, and synagogues are found close together. The photograph on the right shows people outside a kosher bakery (see pages 16–17) in Golders Green, London. Nearby there are also kosher restaurants, fish shops, and grocery stores, and shops selling Jewish objects for the home.

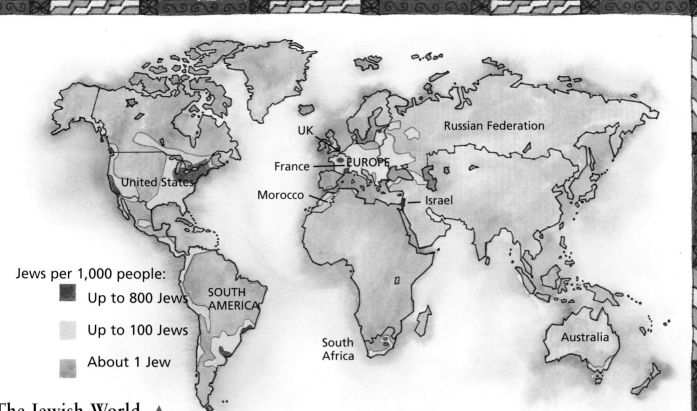

Jews per 1,000 people:

■ Up to 800 Jews

☐ Up to 100 Jews

▨ About 1 Jew

The Jewish World ▲

Israel is the Jewish homeland and Jews have moved there from many countries. It has a Jewish population of 5 million. However, it does not have the world's biggest Jewish population—there are 5.7 million Jews in the United States. Other countries with large Jewish populations include the UK, France, Canada, the Russian Federation, South America, and Australia. Most Jews live in big cities—there are 1.9 million Jews in New York City, for instance.

DIFFERENT IDEAS

Today, there are different ideas about the way Jewish people should live and how they should follow their religion. Jews who still follow all the traditional laws and customs are called Orthodox Jews. Jews who do not follow all the old traditions are called Progressive Jews.

▲ Hasidic Jews

Some Orthodox Jews belong to Hasidic groups. They pray in their own synagogue and send their children to their own schools. They also wear special clothes, like these people who live in Brooklyn, New York.

TIMELINE

EVENTS IN JUDAISM
B.C.E. = Before the Common Era = B.C. (term used by Christians)
C.E. = In the time of the Common Era = A.D.

CREATION	2105 B.C.E.	1813–1653 B.C.E.	1533-1313 B.C.E.	1313 B.C.E.	C.1313–1273 B.C.E.
God creates the world in six days, finishing with man and woman.	God sends great floods. Only Noah, his family, and the animals in the Ark are saved.	Abraham, his son Isaac, and his grandson Jacob start the Jewish religion.	Joseph becomes Viceroy of Egypt. By 1429 B.C.E., his people, the Israelites, have been made into slaves.	God gives the Ten Commandments to Moses but the Israelites disobey God's laws. They are forced to spend 40 years in the wilderness.	Moses dies during the years in the Wilderness. The new leader, Joshua, conquers the Land of Israel.

The Tablets of the Law ▶

Noah's Ark ▲

1290–1496 C.E.	1096–1099 C.E.	499 C.E.	135 C.E.	70 C.E.	63 B.C.E.
Many Jews in Europe are killed or expelled for refusing to become Christians.	Crusaders (Christian soldiers) travel to Jerusalem to free the city from Muslim rule. They kill Jews they meet on the way.	The Talmud, a massive series of discussions of Torah laws and explanations, is completed.	The Romans extinguish an attempt at Jewish independence.. Many Jews flee, or are forced into slavery.	The Second Temple is destroyed by the Romans.	Beginning of Roman domination of Israel. Roman power in the near East is still very fragile.

1492 C.E. onward					
Jewish refugees from Spain welcomed by the sultans of the Ottoman Empire.					

◀ Sir Moses Montefiore

1648 C.E.	1654 C.E.	1656 C.E.	1784–1885 C.E.	1809 C.E.	1881–1905 C.E.
Cossacks kill thousands of Jews in Russia and Poland.	The first Jews settle in New Amsterdam (later named New York).	Jews are allowed to live in England again, many years after being forced to leave.	An English Jew, Sir Moses Montefiore, helps Jews who are suffering hardship all over the world.	The first reformed synagogue is opened in Kassel, Germany.	Jews flee from persecution and poverty in Russia and settle in Western Europe, South America, the U.S.A., and Palestine.

The State of Israel

As you can see in the Timeline, the Jewish land of Israel and the Second Temple in Jerusalem were destroyed in Roman times. Ever since then, Jews have prayed every day for Israel to become the Jewish homeland again and for the Temple to be rebuilt.

During World War II, many Jews were killed or forced to flee from their homes. The United Nations decided that the Jews needed a safe homeland. It decided that Palestine should be split into a Jewish state and an Arab state. On May 14, 1948, the Jewish state of Israel was born.

1258 B.C.E. Under the leadership of Joshua, the settlement of Israel by the Jews is completed.	**C. 1020–1004 B.C.E.** Saul becomes the first king of Israel. He kills himself after his three sons die in battle. David becomes king.	**965–928 B.C.E.** Solomon, David's son, becomes king. God gives him permission to build the Temple.	**960's B.C.E.** The First Temple is completed.
	King David's lyre ▶		**586 B.C.E.** The First Temple is destroyed by the Babylonians. Most Jews are forced to leave Israel and go to Babylon.
166–160 B.C.E. Judah the Maccabee leads a rebellion against the Greeks and regains the Temple. The festival of Hanukkah is established.	**332 B.C.E.** Alexander the Great conquers Egypt and Israel. The Greeks lose control of Israel.	**462–455 B.C.E.** Esther, the Jewish wife of the King of the Persians, uncovers a plot to kill the Jews. The festival of Purim is established.	**C. 515 B.C.E.** The Second Temple is completed, following the Jews' return to Israel.
	◀ Theodore Herzl	Shield of David ▶	
1897 C.E. The First Zionist Congress takes place, led by Theodore Herzl. It decides a Jewish homeland should be set up in Palestine.	**1917 C.E.** The British, who control Palestine at this time, support the setting up of a Jewish homeland in Palestine.	**1939–1945 C.E.** The Nazis kill six million Jews during World War II.	**1948 C.E.** The Jewish state of Israel is set up. Jews from many countries move to Israel to start new lives.

The Shield of David ▲

This six-pointed star is known as the "Shield of David" or the "Seal of Solomon." It has been a special symbol for Jewish people for hundreds of years and it appears on the national flag of Israel.

HOW DID JUDAISM BEGIN?

Jews believe that their religion, Judaism, was started by Abram. According to the Torah, Abram was born around 1813 B.C.E. and married Sarai. Led by

God, they set out on a journey to the land of Canaan. Abram made an agreement, or covenant, with God to be faithful to him and teach his laws to the world. To mark the agreement, Abram circumcised himself. God changed their names to Abraham and Sarah, and promised that their descendants would inherit the Land of Israel.

Worshiping Idols ▼

The people of Canaan worshiped idols—statues of their many gods and goddesses. They made offerings to the idols, so that the gods and goddesses would grant their wishes and, for example, give them victory in battle or a good harvest.

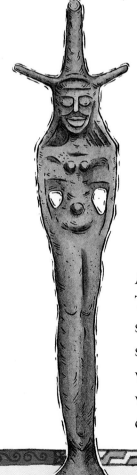

A statue of Astarte, one of the most famous goddesses

Abraham and Isaac ▲

This painting shows a famous scene from the story of Abraham. God told Abraham to sacrifice his son Isaac to him. This was a test to find out how faithful Abraham was to God's commands. Abraham was about to sacrifice the boy when God sent an angel to stop him. Abraham then saw a ram caught in a bush and offered the ram to God instead.

MEDITERRANEAN SEA

Jericho

River Nile

Raamses

Succoth

Elath

RED SEA

Probable route taken by the Israelites ——

Another possible route ......

The Exodus ▲

Joseph's descendants, the Israelites, made their home in Egypt but a new pharaoh began to treat them cruelly. God sent ten plagues on Egypt to show his anger. Eventually, the pharaoh agreed to let Moses, the Israelite leader, take his people away.

Jacob's Dream ▲

Jacob, the son of Isaac, dreamed of a ladder between Earth and Heaven, with angels going up and down. God spoke to Jacob as he lay dreaming and promised to look after him. Jacob said he would be faithful to God and God gave him the name "Israel."

Joseph ▶

Jacob gave a special coat to his favorite son, Joseph. Joseph's jealous brothers sold him as a slave. But in Egypt, he became a powerful man. The story is told in the musical *Joseph and the Amazing Technicolor Dreamcoat.*

THE PARTING OF THE RED SEA

The Pharaoh quickly changed his mind about letting the Israelites go and sent his army after them. It seemed there was no escape for Moses and his people, but God parted the waters of the Red Sea, allowing them to cross in safety. The waters closed again behind them, drowning the Egyptians.

13

WHAT DO JEWS BELIEVE?

All religious Jews believe in the existence of one everlasting and invisible God. They also believe that God chose them to receive the Torah—the first part of the *Tenakh*, the Jewish holy book. By studying the Torah and following its laws, they can spread justice throughout the world. Their good deeds will be rewarded in Heaven. They also believe that the Messiah will come to make this world perfect.

▼ The Ten Commandments

Jews believe that Moses was given the Torah by God on Mount Sinai. He brought back from the mountain the Ten Commandments, carved on pieces (tablets) of stone. The stone tablets were kept in a golden box called the Ark. The Ark was kept in a magnificent tent called the Tabernacle during the Israelites' long journey through the Wilderness from Egypt to Israel.

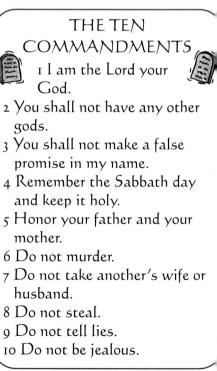

THE TEN COMMANDMENTS

1 I am the Lord your God.
2 You shall not have any other gods.
3 You shall not make a false promise in my name.
4 Remember the Sabbath day and keep it holy.
5 Honor your father and your mother.
6 Do not murder.
7 Do not take another's wife or husband.
8 Do not steal.
9 Do not tell lies.
10 Do not be jealous.

The Six Days of Creation

Jews believe that when God made the world, he created day and night on the first day. On the second day, he separated the heavens from the earth. On the third day, he made the seas, the land, and everything that grows. The Sun, Moon, and stars were created on the fourth day, and the fish and birds on the fifth day. On the sixth day, God created the land, animals, and people.

First day

Second day

Third day

Fourth day

Fifth day

Sixth day

◄ Orthodox Jews

Orthodox Jews try to follow all the laws and customs that have been laid down over centuries. The men in this photograph have long side-curls and beards because they follow certain laws about cutting hair. They are putting cooking pots in water, as part of their preparations for the festival of Pesach. The water is a symbol for purity.

Progressive Jews ►

Progressive Jews believe that religious laws can be changed to reflect the way people live in modern society. For example, they believe that women can become rabbis.

HOW DO JEWISH FAMILIES LIVE?

The Jewish religion plays a very important part in family life. Children learn how to take part in ceremonies from the age of three. They are also taught how to behave toward other people. For example, they

learn that they should respect their parents and help the sick.

The rules about the foods that Jews can eat are set out in the Torah. The food that Jews are allowed to eat is called kosher food.

◀ Mezuzah

This man is fixing a mezuzah to the door frame of his house. The mezuzah is a scroll, usually rolled up inside a case like the one in the drawing (right). The Shema, the most important Jewish prayer, is written on it. The mezuzah reminds people every day of the prayer's message.

Mezuzah

Giving to Charity ▶

Giving money and help to other people is an important Jewish belief. Many families have a charity box at home. Children are often given money to put in the box on Fridays, in honor of Shabbat, the Jewish holy day.

Charity box

Kosher food guide

Kosher Food Guide ▶

Many families use a guide book like the one in the picture to help them make sure they only buy and eat kosher food.

A Kosher Kitchen ▲

Milk and dairy products must not be cooked or eaten with meat. In the kitchen above, meat meals are cooked and cleaned up with the red equipment. The blue equipment is used for dairy foods. There are even separate sinks for washing red and blue equipment.

The Family ▲

The family above is enjoying an outing together. Jewish people think of themselves as belonging to one large family. All Jews are supposed to take care of one another.

Washing Before a Meal ▲

The girl in the picture above is being taught the correct way to wash her hands before a meal. Children learn a lot about the Jewish way of life from their families.

WHAT ARE THE MOST IMPORTANT TIMES IN A JEW'S LIFE?

The four most important stages in Jewish life are birth, reaching adulthood, marriage, and death. Each stage is marked by a religious ceremony, such as a naming ceremony for a baby. These ceremonies are an opportunity for people

to share their happiness or sorrow. They help Jews to feel part of a wider, caring community. Some of the ceremonies are still performed in exactly the same way as when they were first described in the Torah.

JEWISH NAMES

Jews have a first name and a last name, but they also have a Jewish name. This is made up of their own first name, followed by "ben" (which means "son of") or "bat" (which means "daughter of"), and then their parent's first name. So a boy named David whose father is Aaron and mother is Ruth might be named David ben Aaron, or David ben Ruth, or David ben Aaron and Ruth.

Circumcision and Naming ▼

Boys are circumcised when they are eight days old. This is a reminder of the covenant Abraham made with God. Boys are also given their Jewish names at this time. A girl may be named at birth by her father in the synagogue, or at a baby-naming ceremony.

Cushion used at a circumcision ceremony

◄ Bar Mitzvah

Boys become bar mitzvah at the age of 13. This means that they take on the duties of a Jewish adult. One of these duties is to wear tefillin—small boxes containing the Shema prayer and words from the Torah. Many Jews celebrate bar mitzvah by calling the boy up to read from the Torah on Shabbat morning for the first time.

Bat Mitzvah ▶

Girls become bat mitzvah when they are 12 or 13. Progressive Jews, such as the family in the photograph on the right, may celebrate by allowing the girl to read from the Torah.

Marriage ▼

The photograph below shows a formal wedding ceremony in a synagogue. The bride and groom are standing under a canopy—the chuppah—which is a symbol for their new home. Later, the groom will break a glass. This symbolizes the destruction of the two Temples in Jerusalem.

Ceremonial wedding ring

Memorial candle

Death and Mourning

The bodies of Orthodox Jews are always buried. Some Progressive Jewish communities allow cremation. The family of the dead person spends seven days in mourning, and people visit to comfort them. A candle is lit and prayers are said on the anniversary of the death, every year.

WHERE DO JEWS PRAY?

Jews pray anywhere and everywhere! Everyday life is full of opportunities to ask for God's help and blessing—going to bed, getting up, putting on new clothes, eating, drinking, or setting out on a journey. In the synagogue, there are prayers for every occasion.

◀ Bedtime Prayers

This boy is saying his prayers in bed. He is covering his eyes to help him to concentrate. As well as saying the Shema prayer, he will ask God and the angels to protect him while he sleeps.

PRAYER

Jews can pray privately whenever they wish. There are also morning, afternoon, and evening prayers, which should be recited in the synagogue. Orthodox Jews have different views as to which formal prayers women must say.

An Ancient Synagogue ▶

Jews have been praying in synagogues for almost 3,000 years. This synagogue in Tunisia is very old. The men here are wearing the traditional clothes worn by Jews in Arab countries, such as the red hat called a fez.

Orthodox and Progressive Synagogues ▼

Men and women sit together for prayer in a Progressive synagogue, but in an Orthodox synagogue, they sit separately. Sometimes the women sit behind a screen; sometimes they sit upstairs in a balcony.

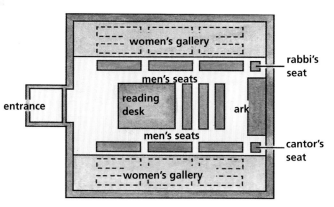

Orthodox synagogue

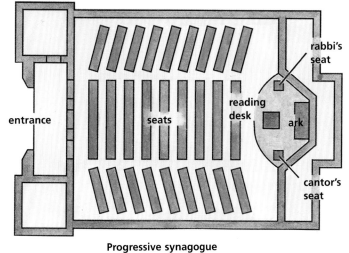

Progressive synagogue

◀ A Modern Synagogue

The spectacular synagogue in the photograph is in Philadelphia, Pennsylvania. A modern synagogue is not only a place where Jews come to pray and study. They can also take part in social events and get help and advice there. It is the center of the Jewish community.

HOW DO JEWS PRAY?

In the synagogue, prayers can be led by the rabbi, by a professional prayer leader called the cantor, or by an ordinary person. In an Orthodox synagogue, prayers can only be led by men or boys age 13 and over.

Orthodox Jews say all their prayers in Hebrew. Progressive Jews might use Hebrew, or their own local language. Jews normally stand or sit to pray. Some prayers, such as the bedtime Shema, should be said last thing at night before going to sleep.

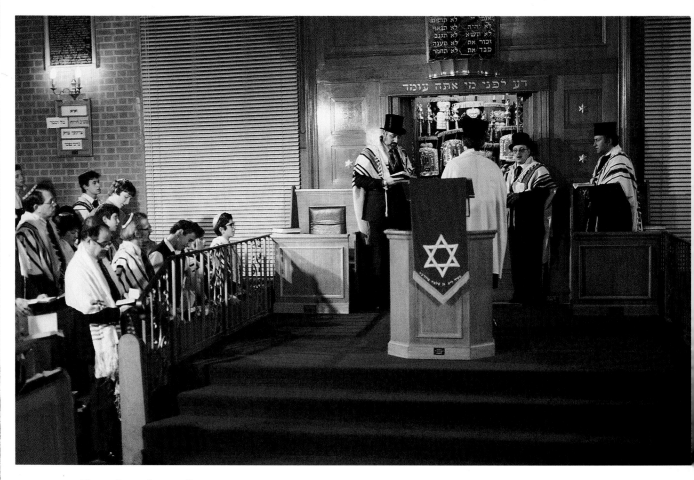

Praying in a Synagogue ▲

This photograph shows a service in an Orthodox synagogue. The cantor has his back to the congregation. He is singing a special prayer as the Torah scrolls are taken out of the Holy Ark. The rabbi is on the far right of the photograph.

Saying the Morning Service ▶

This Orthodox Jewish man is saying the weekday morning service. He is wearing a skull cap called a yarmulke or kippah. He is also wearing tefillin, the two boxes containing lines from the Torah, one on his head and one near his heart. He wears them as a reminder of the message of the Shema prayer.

 THE SHEMA PRAYER

Listen Israel, the Lord is our God, the Lord is one. Let the name of his magnificent kingdom be blessed for ever and ever.

You shall love the Lord your God with all your heart, with all your soul, and with everything you have. Let these words, which I command you today, be on your heart. Teach them carefully to your children. Speak of them when you are sitting at home and when you are traveling, when you go to bed and when you get up. Tie them on your arm as a sign and as tefillin between your eyes. Write them on the doorposts of your house and on your gateposts.

Blessing the Children ▼

Parents bless their children before the meal on Friday evenings and on festival evenings. They ask God to help the children and look after them. There are different blessings for boys and girls.

Praying at Mealtimes ▲

This photograph shows a girl at a Jewish school saying Birkat Hamazon—the Blessings after Meals—in Hebrew. Before their lunch, the children wash their hands in a special way and say a blessing. They make the blessing for bread and then they eat.

WHAT DO JEWS DO ON SHABBAT?

Shabbat is the day of rest. It begins just before sunset on Friday night and lasts until it gets dark on Saturday. Jewish families often invite guests to share meals, songs, stories, prayers, and Torah learning.

They wear their best clothes, light candles, and serve the best food they can afford.
They go to the synagogue and enjoy the break from their everyday activities.

Havdalah candle

Lighting Candles ▲

In this photograph, the mother and her daughters have just lit candles to welcome in Shabbat. They make a sign of welcome over the candles, then cover their eyes to say a blessing. The candles are a symbol of joy and holiness.

ACTIVITIES FORBIDDEN ON SHABBAT

For Orthodox Jews, Shabbat has to be a day of complete rest. They are not allowed to do any of the following: cook; light a fire; switch on electrical equipment; write; watch television; play musical instruments; travel in any type of vehicle; or ride a bicycle. Before Shabbat begins, they have to prepare enough food, light, and heat to last the whole day.

Food for Shabbat

Jews always begin the meal on Friday night and Shabbat lunch by saying blessings over wine and eating two special loaves called challahs. Many traditional recipes were ways of making a little meat or fish feed a lot of people, because Jews were often very poor. Cholent, or *hamim*, for instance, is meat that is stewed with onions, potatoes, and beans over Friday night and Saturday morning, to make a hot meal for lunch.

Challahs

Cholent (hamim)

Chopped herring

Chopped liver

Gefilte fish (fishcake)

Reading the Torah ▶

This photograph shows a rabbi reading from the Torah. The Torah reading is the central part of the morning service on Shabbat. The Torah scroll is the most holy object in the Jewish religion. It is carried to the platform (the bimah) in a solemn procession.

◀ Havdalah

When three stars can be seen in the sky, Shabbat is over for another week. Jews perform a ceremony called Havdalah, to separate the holiness of Shabbat from the ordinary weekday. The photograph on the left shows a father doing this by saying blessings over wine, spices, and a braided candle.

HOW DOES THE JEWISH CALENDAR WORK?

The Jewish calendar is split into 12 months. It is based on the phases of the moon, instead of the movements of the sun. Each month lasts for 29 or 30 days. This means that a Jewish year is about 11 days shorter than a civil year. To make up for this, the calendar has leap years that have an extra month of Adar (January–February).
In a leap year, the normal month of Adar (February–March) is called Adar 2.

THE JEWISH CALENDAR

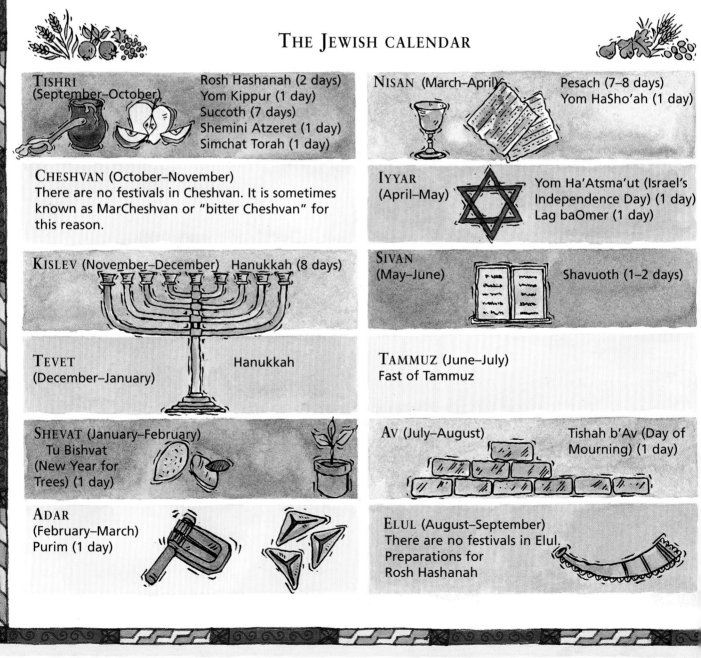

TISHRI (September–October)
Rosh Hashanah (2 days)
Yom Kippur (1 day)
Succoth (7 days)
Shemini Atzeret (1 day)
Simchat Torah (1 day)

CHESHVAN (October–November)
There are no festivals in Cheshvan. It is sometimes known as MarCheshvan or "bitter Cheshvan" for this reason.

KISLEV (November–December) Hanukkah (8 days)

TEVET (December–January) Hanukkah

SHEVAT (January–February)
Tu Bishvat (New Year for Trees) (1 day)

ADAR (February–March)
Purim (1 day)

NISAN (March–April)
Pesach (7–8 days)
Yom HaSho'ah (1 day)

IYYAR (April–May)
Yom Ha'Atsma'ut (Israel's Independence Day) (1 day)
Lag baOmer (1 day)

SIVAN (May–June)
Shavuoth (1–2 days)

TAMMUZ (June–July)
Fast of Tammuz

AV (July–August)
Tishah b'Av (Day of Mourning) (1 day)

ELUL (August–September)
There are no festivals in Elul. Preparations for Rosh Hashanah

◄ Rosh Hashanah and Yom Kippur

Rosh Hashanah is the Jewish New Year and it is celebrated on Tishri 1 and 2 (September–October). Bread and apple, dipped in honey, and honey cake are traditional treats. They symbolize people's hopes for a sweet and happy New Year.

The first ten days of Tishri are known as the Ten Days of Penitence. People ask God to forgive them and pray for a new start in life. The shofar (ram's horn) is blown. This is to wake up people's conscience. Yom Kippur, the most solemn festival, is on Tishri 10.

Yom Ha'Atsma'ut ▲

The State of Israel was created by the United Nations on May 14, 1948. This date is a national holiday in Israel and celebrations are held in Jewish communities throughout the world. You can see people waving Israeli flags in the photograph above.

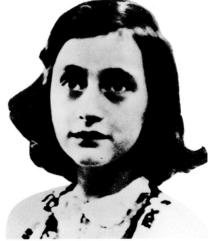

Yom HaSho'ah ▲

Anne Frank, shown above, was just one of the six million Jews who were killed by the Nazis before and during World War II (1939–45). On Nisan 27, Jews around the world hold ceremonies in honor of the victims.

WHAT ARE THE THREE PILGRIM FESTIVALS?

In ancient times, Jews made pilgrimages to Jerusalem to make offerings at the Temple on three festivals. At Pesach or Passover, they celebrated the Exodus from Egypt by making an offering of a lamb. At Shavuoth, they offered some of the first crops from the harvest. At Succoth, they made offerings to mark the end of the harvest. Today, there is no Temple but Jews celebrate these festivals at home and in the synagogue.

Pesach ▶

This plate is used for the Seder service in Jewish homes at Pesach. Each of the foods has a special meaning. The bone is a symbol of the Pesach lamb. The burned egg symbolizes the festival offering. Next to the bone is bitter horseradish, which symbolizes the bitter life of the Israelites in Egypt. *Charoset*, the spicy nut mixture beside the egg, symbolizes the mortar used to build the pyramids. Next comes salt water, for the tears of the Israelites, and green vegetables. Matzo, the unleavened bread eaten by the Israelites, is also an important part of the service.

Shavuoth ▶

Shavuoth is celebrated seven weeks after Pesach. It marks the time when God gave the Torah to Moses on Mount Sinai. It is also the Festival of the First Fruits. These children are on an Israeli kibbutz celebrating the gathering of the first crops from the harvest. Dairy foods such as cheesecake are traditionally eaten at this festival.

Succoth ▼

The family in this photograph is eating in the temporary hut, or succah, they have built for Succoth. The roof is made of branches and is open to the sky. People build huts like this to remember how God protected the Israelites in their fragile homes in the Wilderness.

THE HARVEST

Seven types of food were harvested in Israel—wheat, barley, grapes, olives, pomegranates, dates, and figs. Many Jews hang up each type of food in the succah.

The Lulav and Etrog ▼

The *lulav* is a palm leaf, which is tied in a bundle with willow and myrtle branches. The *etrog* is a fruit like a lemon. The *lulav* bundle and the *etrog* are used in special blessings and ceremonies held during Succoth.

Lulav

Etrog

ARE THERE ANY OTHER JEWISH FESTIVALS?

Purim and Hanukkah are two festivals that mark miraculous events when God helped the Jews. Tu Bishvat, the New Year for Trees, is often

marked by the planting of new trees. These three festivals were described in the encyclopedia of Torah laws (the Talmud) before 500 C.E. Simchat Torah, the Festival of Rejoicing in the Torah, was introduced several hundred years later.

Simchat Torah ▲

Simchat Torah is celebrated when the yearly reading of the Torah texts is complete. The scrolls are taken out of the Holy Ark. In the photograph above, you can see people carrying them in a procession around the synagogue. Simchat Torah is a joyous occasion.

THE TORAH

The Torah is made up of five books—the Five Books of Moses. Each book is divided into sections called *sidrot*. At least one section is read every Shabbat, so that the whole of the Torah can be read each year.

◀ Hanukkah

Hanukkah celebrates the time when the Jews recaptured the Temple from the Greeks. There was only enough holy oil to keep the seven-branched candlestick (the menorah) burning for one day. Miraculously, it lasted for eight days, until more oil could be prepared. People eat food cooked in oil at this festival.

Potato *latkes*

Doughnuts

Olive oil

Tu Bishvat ▶

To mark the New Year for Trees, people often plant trees that are mentioned in the *Tenakh*, the Jewish bible. These Israeli girls are soldiers at work on a farm. It is traditional to eat 15 different types of fruit because Tu Bishvat is celebrated on Shevat 15.

◀ Purim

Purim celebrates the story of Esther who saved the Jews from a plot to kill them. When the story is read, people make a lot of noise to blot out the name of the villain, Haman. They enjoy triangular-shaped pastries called hamantaschen. The photograph on the left shows people dressed up for Purim.

Wine

Hamantaschen

WHAT ARE THE JEWS' HOLY BOOKS?

The Five Books of Moses are written on the Torah scroll. The Torah is the holiest Jewish book and it forms the first part of the *Tenakh*, the Jewish bible. The second part is the *Nev'im*—the books of th Prophets. The third part is the *Ketuvim* and this includes Psalms, Proverbs, and five special stories or poems linked to festivals. The Talmud (the books of Torah laws) and prayer books are the other holy books.

▼ The Torah Scroll

The Torah scroll is wound on two wooden rollers. This one is held inside a richly decorated wooden case. Some Torah scrolls are held in an embroidered cover, decorated with silver bells and crowns.

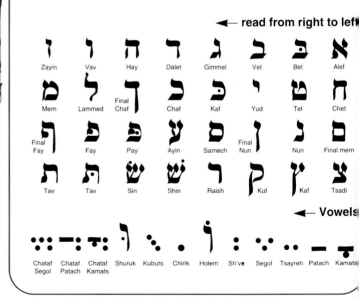

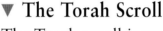
THE HEBREW ALPHABET

The *Tenakh* is written in Hebrew. The Hebrew spoken in Israel today is similar to the Hebrew used in the Torah. You can see the Hebrew characters below.

← read from right to left

Zayin	Vav	Hay	Dalet	Gimmel	Vet	Bet	Alef
Mem	Lammed	Final Chaf	Chaf	Kaf	Yud	Tet	Chet
Final Fay	Fay	Pay	Ayin	Samech	Final Nun	Nun	Final mem
Tav	Tav	Sin	Shin	Raish	Kuf	Kaf	Tsadi

← Vowels

Chataf Segol	Chataf Patach	Chataf Kamats	Shuruk	Kubuts	Chirik	Holem	Sh'va	Segol	Tsayreh	Patach	Kamats

The Haggadah ▲

The Haggadah contains the prayers, service, and songs for the Pesach Seder. In many families, each person has their own copy of the Haggadah. The one in the photograph above is designed for children to use. The Haggadah is one of the oldest Jewish books. Copies still exist that are more than 500 years old.

◄ The Scribe

Torah scrolls and mezuzah scrolls (see page 16) have to be handwritten. The photograph on the left shows a scribe writing the words of the Shema prayer on a mezuzah scroll. He has to use a quill pen, with ink made to an ancient recipe. He writes on specially prepared parchment and there are strict rules about how to write each word. It takes about a year to write a Torah scroll.

WHO ARE THE JEWISH LEADERS?

From the earliest days of their religion, the Jews believed that the men and women who led them were prophets chosen by God. Later, when the Israelites were settled in Israel, their leaders included

judges and kings. Today, rabbis are the Jews' religious leaders. Orthodox Jews believe that only men can be rabbis, but Progressive Jews allow women to become rabbis, too.

◄ **Saul and David**

Saul was the first king of Israel. He suffered from depression but he was comforted by the harp music played by David, the best friend of his son Jonathan. David became king after Saul. He is famous for the psalms he composed and for making Jerusalem his capital city.

✦ PROPHETS ✦

There were many prophets who were leaders. Moses, Aaron, Miriam, and Joshua led the Israelites through the Wilderness to the Land of Israel. They tried to get people to follow God's laws and treat each other well.

Maimonides ▶

This picture shows Maimonides, who was also known as Rabbi Moses ben Maimon or Rambam. He was born in Spain in the twelfth century C.E. but moved to Egypt to escape religious persecution. He was one of the greatest medieval rabbis and his books are still read today.

◀ Training to Be a Rabbi

These young men are studying holy books at a *yeshiva*—a training college for rabbis. People have to study for many years to become rabbis. Today, many Orthodox and all Progressive rabbis study at universities for degrees. Modern rabbis also learn skills such as public speaking.

A *Sephardi* rabbi

The Rabbi as Leader ▲

This is Rabbi Dr. Jonathan Sacks presenting a certificate to a new rabbi. Rabbi Dr. Sacks is the Chief Rabbi of the United Synagogues of Britain, and leads the largest group of Jews in the UK. In Israel, there are two chief rabbis. One leads the Ashkenazi community of Western and European Jews. The other leads the Sephardi community of Spanish, Portuguese, and Oriental Jews.

WHICH ARE THE JEWS' HOLY PLACES?

The holiest place for Jews was the Temple built by King Solomon on Mount Moriah in Jerusalem. That Temple was destroyed by the Babylonians. The Second Temple was destroyed by the Romans. The Western Wall is the only part of it that remains. Other holy places include the Mount of Olives in Jerusalem and the burial sites of Jewish leaders. The tomb of Rabbi Maimonides (see page 34), for example, is at Tiberias.

The Western Wall ▲

Jews come from all over the world to visit the Western Wall (also known as the Wailing Wall) because it is the last surviving part of the holy Temple. They come to pray, and they push pieces of paper with prayers and requests between the stones. As you can see in the photograph above, the area in front of the Wall is divided by a screen so that men and women can pray separately.

36

The Mount of Olives ▲

Jews believe that when the Messiah comes, he will bring the dead back to life. He will enter Jerusalem from the Mount of Olives. The people buried there will be the first to follow him to the Eternal Kingdom of God.

 CAVE OF MACHPELAH

The Cave of Machpelah is in Hebron. Adam and Eve, Abraham and Sarah, Isaac and Rebekkah, and Jacob and Leah were buried there, according to tradition. Rachel, Jacob's favorite wife, was buried in Bethlehem.

Jerusalem

Jerusalem is the Jews' holiest city because the two Temples stood there. However, it is also a holy city for Christians and Muslims. It has been fought over for centuries, because followers of each religion wanted the city only for themselves.

MEDITERRANEAN SEA

LEBANON

Tiberias

SEA OF GALILEE

River Jordan

Jerusalem
Bethlehem

Hebron

DEAD SEA

ISRAEL

EGYPT

JORDAN

GULF OF ARABIA

Sites of Jewish holy places

WHAT ARE THE JEWISH RITUAL OBJECTS?

Almost every Jewish activity has a religious object linked to it. For example, people might keep a special jug for washing their hands before a meal. They might have a different jug, made of more expensive materials or with more decoration, that they use only on Shabbat or for the festivals. Ritual objects are made of the best materials the owner can afford.

◄ The Holy Ark and the Torah Scrolls

The photograph on the left shows the holy Torah scrolls inside the Holy Ark. The scrolls at the back of the Ark may be too old to use any more, but they are still looked after carefully. The scrolls that are used have silver breastplates, pointers and bells, or crowns, as well as embroidered covers.

SPICE BOXES

The Havdalah ceremony marks the end of Shabbat. As part of the ceremony, a box of spices is passed around for each person to smell. This is to refresh their souls for the week ahead. The spice boxes have beautiful designs and decorations.

Torah Pointers ▶

The Torah scroll must not be touched by hand, so people use pointers to help them keep to the right line as they are reading.

Noisemaker

Noisemakers ▲

Noisemakers are used to blot out the name of the villain, Haman, when the story of Esther is read at Purim.

Silver pointers

◀ Spinning Tops

The dreidel, or *sevivon*, is a spinning top used at Hanukkah. It has four Hebrew letters on it, which stand for "A Great Miracle Happened There."

Dreidels

Marriage Certificate ▲

Marriage certificates are often handwritten and beautifully decorated, like the one in the photograph above. Some people have them on display in their home.

The Eternal Light ▶

The photograph on the right shows the *Ner Tamid*, or Eternal Light. It hangs in front of the Holy Ark in the synagogue. It is a symbol of the menorah that was kept burning all the time in the Temple. It is also a reminder that the Torah is the guiding light of the Jews.

IS MUSIC IMPORTANT IN JUDAISM?

Music-making has been important since ancient times. Musical instruments were made especially for use in the Temple. Orthodox synagogues do not use musical instruments on Shabbat or on festival days. The only music they allow is singing. Many Progressive synagogues do use musical instruments in their services. Folk songs are important in Jewish communities, too.

Miriam and the Women ▶

Moses made up a hymn to thank God after the Egyptian soldiers chasing the Israelites were drowned in the Red Sea. Miriam took the women off to dance and sing the hymn on their own. The painting on the right shows Miriam playing her timbrel.

Trumpet

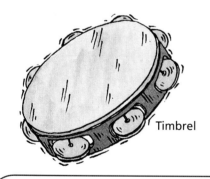
Timbrel

Cymbals

MUSIC IN THE TENAKH

Many musical instruments are mentioned in the *Tenakh*. The most famous are Miriam's timbrel, which is a type of tambourine; King David's lyre, which is a small harp; and the ram's horn, or shofar. A famous story tells how the sound of the shofar brought down the walls of the city of Jericho. Harps, lyres, cymbals, flutes, and trumpets were played in the Temple.

◄ Wedding Music

Music is very important at Jewish weddings. There are special tunes for psalms and hymns, and beautiful music written especially for use at weddings. A cantor or choir often escorts the bride to the wedding canopy. At the wedding meal, the couple are entertained with happy songs.

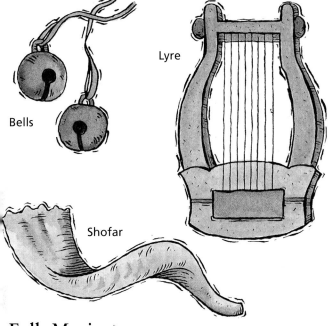

Bells

Lyre

Shofar

Folk Music ►

Folk songs are a way of passing on the traditions of Jewish people. Some songs and folk dances come from the *Tenakh*. Others come from countries where Jews have lived for centuries, such as Russia. Folk dancing, as shown in the photograph on the right, is popular at all kinds of celebrations.

ARE STORIES IMPORTANT TO JEWISH PEOPLE?

People have always used stories to pass down the Jewish laws and traditions from one generation to another. Many of the important ideas in the Jewish holy books about how people should live their lives

are explained in stories. At the Pesach Seder service, the whole family sits around the table, telling stories. They tell the story of the Jews' slavery in Egypt, how God sent the Ten Plagues, and how the Jews eventually escaped from Egypt.

◀ **Jonah and the Big Fish**
The book of Jonah the Prophet, from the *Tenakh*, teaches people about being sorry and about forgiveness. It tells how Jonah disobeyed God and tried to escape from him. The ship he was traveling in was hit by a storm. Jonah was thrown overboard and swallowed by a giant fish. Jonah prayed to God for forgiveness and was thrown up on land.

SAYINGS AND PROVERBS

The Jewish holy books contain many wise sayings that are still used today. Here are some examples:

"Do not judge a man until you have stood in his place."

"A fool says what he knows, a wise man knows what he says."

"God gave man one mouth and two ears so that he could listen twice as much as he could speak."

Rabbi Akiva

Rabbi Akiva (50–135 C.E.) was one of the greatest rabbis of his time. He told many stories to comfort his followers and give them courage in the difficult times they lived in.

Akiva ben Joseph was a poor shepherd boy but he fell in love with his wealthy master's daughter, Rachel. Rachel agreed to marry him but only if he became a Torah scholar. Her father was so angry about their marriage that he refused to give them a penny. They were so poor that Rachel had to sell her hair to buy food.

Eventually, Akiva became a great scholar but he lived at a time when the Jews were being persecuted by the Romans. The Romans burned him to death for teaching the Torah.

Children Listening to a Story ▲

Stories help people to understand what being Jewish means. These children may be listening to a Torah story, or a new story about their faith.

The Torch, the Cockerel, and the Donkey

Once, Rabbi Akiva went on a journey, riding on a donkey. He took with him a cockerel to wake him in the morning and a burning torch to light his way in the dark. When he came to a village, he asked for a bed for the night but everyone turned him away. Instead of being angry, he accepted it as God's will and went to sleep in a field.

During the night, a lion killed the donkey, a fox ate the cockerel, and the torch blew out. Next morning, Rabbi Akiva discovered that robbers had attacked the village and killed all the people. "If I had stayed in the village," he said, "I would have been killed, too. The robbers might even have seen my torch if it had not blown out, or heard my donkey and cockerel, and found me in the field. I see now that everything is in God's hand."

43

GLOSSARY

Ark of the Covenant The place where the tablets on which the Ten Commandments were written were kept in ancient times; the Holy Ark is the place where the Torah scrolls are kept in the synagogue.

bar mitzvah A Jewish boy becomes bar mitzvah at the age of 13; this means he takes on the responsibilities of an adult within Judaism. A ceremony is held to mark the occasion.

bat mitzvah A ceremony with a similar meaning to Bar Mitzvah (see above), held when a girl reaches the age of 12 or 13.

circumcision Removal of the loose skin (the foreskin) at the tip of the penis.

Exodus The departure of the Israelites, led by Moses, from Egypt.

Hebrew The language used in the *Tenakh*, and also in modern Israel.

Israelites The name given to people descended from Jacob, who was given a new name, "Israel," by God.

kosher Food that the Torah lists as being suitable for Jews to eat. It includes all fruit and vegetables; fish that have scales and fins, such as cod; animals that chew the cud and have split hooves, such as cows; and certain types of bird, including chickens.

menorah A candlestick with eight branches.

Messiah The long-awaited deliverer of the Jews.

Pesach (Passover) The festival that marks the time when God sent the tenth plague on the Egyptians—the death of their first-born sons— but spared ("passed over") the Israelites. This led to the Exodus of the Israelites from Egypt.

pilgrimage A journey to a holy place.

prophets People who speak the words of God.

psalms Religious songs.

ritual An activity that has to be performed in a certain way, and has a religious meaning.

Shabbat The Jewish holy day, when Jews rest from their normal activities.

synagogue The building used by Jews for worship.

Tabernacle A magnificent tent, in which the Ark of the Covenant was kept during the Israelites' journey through the Wilderness.

Talmud An encyclopedia of Jewish laws and explanations of the Torah, dictated to Moses by God on Mount Sinai but not written down for many centuries.

tefillin Two small square boxes that contain the Shema prayer and other words from the Torah. They are attached to the head and arm by leather straps.

temple The first Temple was built on Mount Moriah by King Solomon. The two stone tablets with the Ten Commandments written on them were kept there. It was the holiest place for prayer and making sacrifices until it was destroyed by the Babylonians. The second Temple was destroyed by the Romans.

Tenakh The Jewish bible.

Ten Commandments The ten instructions given to Moses by God on Mount Sinai, which set out how Jews should live.

Torah The first five books of the *Tenakh*, which were dictated to Moses by God.

unleavened bread Bread made without yeast, so it does not rise.

wilderness The desert lands through which the Israelites wandered on their journey from Egypt to the Promised Land of Israel.

FURTHER READING

Judaism
by Ian Graham
(Walrus Books, 2005)

Portraits of Jewish American Heroes
by Malka Drucker
(Dutton Juvenile, 2008)

World Religions: Judaism
by Natalie M Rosinsky
(Compass Point Books, 2009)

INDEX

WEB SITES

Due to the changing nature of Internet links, Rosen Publishing has developed an online list of Web sites related to the subject of this book. This site is updated regularly. Please use this link to access this list: http://www.rosenlinks.com/wrel/juda